I VS THE WORLD

I VS THE WORLD

POETRY OF LOVE & EXISTENCE FROM A CONCENTRIC PERSPECTIVE

Ed Choi

ISBN-13: 9780985867102
ISBN-10: 0985867108
Library of Congress Control Number: 2015910067
Ed Choi Publishing, Los Angeles, CA

I dedicate this book

To my beloved wife,

Joy

Of over 3 score years together

Through pains and pleasures of life

Now reaching

The height of our happiness

As great grand parents

We are bound in love

Forever

TABLE OF CONTENTS

PART I: PROLOGUE

PREFACE

A time to wind down everything
Before too late
A will to the survivors is due
My own will to my family and beyond
I wish to leave a legacy of living
A happy long life
For this enduring happiness of my life
I owe God
A way of life
In happiness and health
Even now at my age, 84
I owe little to the world
But everything to the Love of God

An existential philosopher
Or any such pursuers
Would even envy the state of my life
As this old man's health and happiness sparkle
The wisdoms of men, even of great men
Are only the derivatives of
Love and Truth

Most people love the things of the world
And flirt with their own ideas
But I keep my heart and tune into Truth
And love the things of God with all my heart

Their hearts flirt with their ideas
And, out of the heart
Are the issues of life on hand

The world conditions a man
To be a part of the whole
And wear him down into pieces
Eventually, even onto death!

In order to pursue a way of life for
A happy wholesome life
One has to choose one's destination
I chose God over the World
For the journey of Faith
Away from the human bondage of
The sense-based world value

Why God over the world?
In addition to Pascal's wager
I have even stronger reasons
To choose God
I am convinced that God is Love
St. John, the beloved disciple of Jesus
Says in the Bible
God is Love (1 John 4: 8, 16)
And I believe
Love is the essence of life
The wellsprings of life
Empowering the existence

The Love flows from God
Perpetually flowing from Him
Into our drowsy soul

Calling to wake it up to the Love
I therefore gasp after God's Love

On the other hand
From my own perspective
The world is the thing of the eyes and ears
And the flickering lights
No depth nor stability at all
Only the fleeting permanent illusion!
No more than the Flux in Greek term
That devours the individual
With ever increasing appetites
And grows in the power
Amalgamating them all
The being of the individual sinks and
Suffers the fate

God is the ground of being
His Love is the staple of life
As important as the air we breathe for the body
As the love is for the soul
Which owns the body

My soul yearns for God's Love
I work hard to earn His Love
With all diligence
Even in my dreams

May God bless all the readers of this book
With His Love

Amen

SALUTE TO LOVE

I salute Love with my book:
"I vs the World"
I adore, even worship the Love as God's

To be or not to be:
This is not the question
But it is to choose one or the other
To be a beloved, or
To be a lover
This is the real question
To love is to be
To love is to survive a life
To survive the life itself
In the ever amalgamating, and hardening whole
Which is called "the world?"
And to avoid becoming just a particle of the whole
And to keep the self as an integral whole
The individual integrity matters

A life is to choose one or the other:
Either to be a lover or to be a beloved
The beloved vs the lover
For love is the most essential for a life
As essential as water is to the body
The soul of the body perishes without it

As a plant dies in a drought
How, then, does this love come to a life?
Through loving others and caring for them
As God rewards a lover!

The world has superseded the love
With its own love
A man is sandwiched between two poles:
The world on the left, and God on the right.
Through man's senses and ego
The world controls the man
On the opposite pole, which is on the right
God perceives all things
But He implants His Pole of Love on the right
And reigns over man's soul
Thus, man is in between:
The material master on the left
And spiritual master on the right

The world begets the beloved
And raises them with the things of the world
Only to eat them up
Or behead them with its whims
Littering the backyard with the corpses
In a funk of the world
The beloved teeters
On the edge of the cliff!!

Who then Is my own Enemy?
Much search for all my adversaries:
Far and wide; from the obvious to the most obscure;
From what the eye can see
To what the mind can think of

I still have no idea of what they really are
All I know is that they exist to destroy me
I can't pinpoint who is my real enemy
How can I find and go after them?
The prodigy of pondering drags me on.

Then, in a trance deeper than dream
I heard the gasping of my soul,
Sounding like the least note of the scale,
Yet clearer than the eardrum itself
Alas! In the wake I now know the enemy is within me,
To destroy the very source of life: my soul.
I cry out in the whirling heart of a master less being!

The soul tunes into the heart beat of being;
The mind dances with the drumbeat of the world.
It is the mind that projects me from my center
Into the black hole of desires; wherein I choke, sink.
It is the mind that is like a heavy magnet,
Attracting crooked nails and pins,
Which further invite the likes;
Wear out my sanity.
What is it? Where is it from?

It is an envoy posted in me by the world,
Who sits on the center of my being
Steals the "I" from me
Like a convict before being beheaded,
The soul shivers and trembles.

But, even now as ever is;
To surrender to this alien agent, and revel with him

To be a beloved
Or to rebel against him
To be cast out, and hauled to the ground
That is the question.

Now that I know my enemy is within me
Who manipulates my life to be a beloved of the world
Oh, "wretched man that I am!
Who shall deliver me
From the body of this death?"

No more choice left for me
But only jump ship to be a lover for good
I am now a free lover for good causes
Walking on the solid ground
To work the works of Love
With God guiding me on the way to Truth

True love transcends common sense and logic
Even the long cherished cultures
Love transcends even the whole things of the world
Loving others is the best tool for self-preservation
Love wins for the self to live in peace and freedom
The world of the lovers is a paradise itself regained
For the individual being
From the enslaving, amalgamating, monster
Which is called "the world"

For this very love; I have, therefore, chosen to be a lover
And have tried to live as a lover for most of my life
I am now living it
I am a live working lab for testing the love!!

Love is being tested through living it
Experimenting, experiencing, digging secret paths
Finding the way to Truth to be a wholesome person

Now, at 84
Still living the life ever vigorously
Lacking nothing; filled with Joy and hope
Enthusiasm overflows with Love, and for love
Looking forward to continuing the work of Love
The lover loves the others for the sake of love
Because he believes in God, which is Love
Love returns invisible to him:
Touching and tingling his sleepy organs
All the cells of the body dance for joy
Rejoice in the harmony and beauty of being a whole person

While the world fragments the mind
The Love defragments it, and synchronizes
Puts back into a loving mode
The loving power grows and
Even becomes innate and naturally
Flowing through the lover
Springing up to enhance and to empower
The existence of the lover himself
Everything else is in the world
Exhaustible, and extinguished in time
But, Love grows and multiplies for the lover
And also for those, whom he loves
That is the real magic
A thing like it is never found in the whole world
Love is the positive force of life
Against the negative power of diseases and death
Love leads to harmony and beauty

Then to Truth, and frees man
Love calms inner turmoil and leads
To peace and hope
It is the anti-sins vaccine
All-ills curing agent
Love is the only bridge
To God, and to an eternal life!

The beloved loves the world
Rides high on the cloud with ever shifting winds
The thunder of cheers just passed through her ears
The glittering glamour fades as soon as she blinks
These things just pass through the ego of the mind
Leaving nothing behind at all
For her heart and soul
The feeling of vanity sets in
And the fear of losing them all
Keeps the soul awake and trembling at night

She is freaked to be a beloved
She finds that there is little love for her
No enduring real love for her
Only at the mercy or whims of the crowd
She seeks an audience, a captive one
Toils to build ever larger ones in vain
Pushed up to be a beloved
Instead, she becomes a tagged merchandise
Being traded as a thing, not as a person
Real love seldom emerges from interaction with the mass
Only from direct personal contacts

A beloved buys love with tears and toils
And with heart and soul

But the love the world gives is only collective
Winds and whims
Never enduring real love
Which is the dream of every person
Just a flickering fantasy!

Audiences are like the winds blowing in the forest
A taller tree bears the greater burdens to bear
As the fetes end, the yard is littered
The heart empty even in the midst
And in the wake of the tumults
The soul crying in loneliness
She teeters on the very edge of her being

On the other side of life
The lover sells love freely
For Love flows to the lover
As he only believes that
God is Love!!

Of a life, love is the linchpin
Love is an essence itself for a being
Love is the home of a human being
Love frees man from slavery
Love implements a life
With health and happiness
A man breathes love to exist
A vital staple for the Mind
Love is the only power to overcome
Fatal fissure in the mind
A human being is what he makes of himself
How is he going about making of himself?

Now, listen to Leo Tolstoy:
"And all people live, not by reason of any care they have for themselves,
But by the love for them
That is in other people."
This very love in the other people
Buds up slowly in their hearts
God sows it using the lovers
All people live for being loved
Love comes to lovers
Only to the lover who gives love freely to others
For he believes that God is Love

Love affects both Mind and Matter
Brings them together
Unifier of the two
Defying the odds and description
Love overcomes the fatal disease
Stealth disease of losing the self to the whole!

Hail to a true lover!!
A true lover rejoices in happiness and health
Enjoying the power of love
Beholding the beauty of Truth
Living a life like no other way

Pay homage to the true lover
As he is a warrior for Love
A peace maker
For the good of the whole
As a benefactor of the whole
Spreading the good virus of Love
For the mankind to be a true lover

Love begets life, and
Bears fruits of it
Love is indeed all things to me
Love functions as my boss

It is now the time to declare
That Love is the most essential force
For existence and for the being

With that all said, I declare that
I dedicate
My life to Love

WHAT IS LOVE?

What is the most intimate thing
To all human beings, and yet
The least understood?
Love!!
Love is like a wind
That touches the skin
And passes by; but
The body braces, and
The spirit embraces it

Love is one-winged
Seeking the other half
To be a whole
Becomes a two-winged entity
Flying freely in/out of Time/space
For a life, and the being of that life
To be
A value of the Invariables
In the midst of Flux
The soul, which owns the life
Is but helpless

Only Love tames the mind
Helps the existence
To be a self-sufficient being

Caring of the body/mind/soul
All together for the being of a life
That Love embodies the being of a life
Empowers it to exist for good!
If death be the negative factor
Let love be the positive force for Life
It lives within the existence
Leads the being in Good and Beauty
Lights the way to Truth

Love is real
Pushing and pulling a life
To be a being
Lifting him up high to see beauty
As well as keeping him down low
For the being with others on the ground
A splendid lateral manifestation!

The love reins the mind
Overcomes the ills of life
It is only the positive renewing force
For existence, period
Two kinds of Love:
Object-driven and subject-driven
A linear love is
An object-driven eccentric force
Toward the magnetic pole of the world
Where all the pomp and pretensions pull
A man out of the self
The glare and glamor so faze him to death

A loop love is the other:
It is the only true love

For it is a subject-driven concentric power
Circling the core of the self
To be one for a whole being
Connected with Truth
Making him a lover
He lives or dies for the Love
The Love begets him to be a true lover
Love flows through him laterally
Like a green mountain stream
It propagates quietly
Peace and serenity prevail
The love fetes the life!

The Truth is that God works through Love
Which is His invisible emissary at large
Seeking the true lovers

After all
God is love

WHO IS MY ENEMY?

Much search for my enemy:
Far and wide; from the obvious to the most obscure;
From what the eye can see,
To what the mind can think of;
I still have no idea of what it really is.
All I know is that it exists to destroy me.
Still, the enemy eludes me.
How can I find and go after it?
The prodigy of pondering drags me on.

Then, in a trance deeper than dream
I heard the gasping of my soul,
Sounding like the least note of the scale,
Yet clearer than the eardrum itself.
Alas! In the wake I now know the enemy is within me,
To destroy the very source of life: my soul.
I cry out in the whirling heart of a masterless being!

The soul tunes into the heart beat of being;
The mind dances with the drumbeat of the men's march.
It is the mind that projects me from my center
Into the black hole of desires; wherein I choke, sink.
It is the mind that is like a heavy magnet,
Attracting crooked nails and pins,
Which further invite the likes;

Wear out my sanity.
What is it? Where is it from?

It is an envoy posted in me by the world,
Who sits on the center of my being;
Steals the "I" from me.
Like a convict before being beheaded,
The soul shivers and trembles.

But, even now as ever is;
To surrender to this alien agent, and revel with him;
Or to rebel against him:
That is the question.

GOD AND NO GOD

Between God and no God
Man stands
Seeking the reference point

Between the sanities of the individual
And the vanities of the whole,
The soul searches its source.

Between Hope and death
Life's ultimate prize
Awaits the man

Since Hope granted or denied
Is never to be experienced
Hope is the eternal Means to the End
Absolute Probability
Never to be disproved,
Hope is real as the breath
As concrete as the sound of the footsteps
Hope hears the pulse of the self and
Overcomes the fears

Can the Mind mired in the Matter
See Hope, which springs from the spirit?
If not I that vow to life, what will?

If not I that sow Hope, who will?
If not in my spirit, where is it to be?

Lest the world causes me wilder my way
Lest I depart from what I am
Refusing to fall to the dearth of will
I rise to Life through Hope

PART II: POETRY

NATURE

A GOLFER

A golfer drills to touch reality
The flesh sweats

The rainbow bridges the mind to Matter
The mind leads the body

The courtship of mind/body begets the reality
The duet performs life

He dreams of a shot streaking for the flag
He labors to deliver it

He loves a sweat swipe at the ball
His pride flies higher than the shot

He drops putts into the holes
His ego soars like an eagle

The thrills hook him on the game
He tastes a slice of life

A SPECTATOR

On the scorched leaves of old trees
The rain pounds
The red muddy water
Trickles down to the pond
That has no drain

The ugly shadows that dot the earth
Take refuge in the night's darkness
The train races roaring
To the night city like an African herd
Over the cliff, a nightmare hangs upside down
A black flying fox clings onto the edge.

From a distant hill
The wood gong sounds
Echoing through the valley
To the city of Light
The full moon shines
Above the sea of things

In the serenity of peace
The spectator's heart beats
Slower and stronger than the ego, and
Pumps life even to the corner of the mind and
To the outermost edge of the body

AFTER THE SUMMER

How lush the summer gives
To all living things!

I am sad the mighty summer
Is about to wane
In the cycles of Season
We shall miss the lusty summer's days

But, remember the fall is even better
For we reap the fruits of our labor
In the hot pursuit
All the summer long

Under the vast, blue sky of the fall
We shall take a deep breath and
Bask in the declining Sun
We all together lift our heads
To the Heaven, and say
Hallelujah!!

BEYOND THE SEASON

To wish to be in the midst of all things
And in the season means riding the Flux
And feeling the pulse of the Mass
As if an attached part is to the Whole

Seasons can come and go
Day or night can be what they wish
Hot or cold: be what it may
What I desire, more than a season
Or even a success, is the comfort
Of feeling the freedom
Beyond the seasons and space
Without form or fashion

Outside the time domain
Watching a leaf falling from a tree
Listening to a group of birds
Singing in sync. Or, say
The dark shadow of Earth
Piles on piles of the dead on the beach
After a Stunami. Worse yet
Blood soaking killing fields
Of the wars. Or, one soul going insane
With a nuke on his hand

And yet, still in perspective
Would perceive them all
Project and steer the self through
I could gain the whole of my being

EMBRACE THE DAWN

To embrace the Dawn
I march East, with my eager feet
Tramping toward the Dawn
Like a lover meeting the beloved
The heart rejoices, and
Leads the way
To the midwife of the Light

In that darkness
And chill of the early hour
My joy overflows
And I adore quietude and peace

Praise the Lord!
The Light is about to be born
Before the mind swooned
In the human "petties" of the day
I am free from filthiness of the flesh
And released from the wicked mind
I drink a sweet savor of the spirit
The heart is being enlarged
Fully energized, I am now ready
To bear a day of the world
Through the dusk

THE LITTERED BEACH & THE SOILED MOON

The beach littered, the moon soiled
And then, the man himself: wretched

The man spoils the Nature and Himself
His own "inners-cape" littered much worse
Than the visible trash
Man indeed corrupts creation
There is no good in him at all

Before he was on the scene
The full virgin moon would visit, and
Embrace the beach kissing with the big waves
Good and beauty then

And now, after having raped the moon
He himself is being lost; Immersed and amalgamated into
The Whole, which he worships as
The icon of the Final March

Am I not also one of the Whole?
Not as a whole being of the individual entity
But, only a part of the Whole
Chained and leeched to the Train of the Whole
Called Singularity
I disappear into it

Like a tributary into the river
Diversity deduced, reduced to Singularity!
All on board head for
The fatal fall into the Matter

An enslaved man that I am
A chained prisoner that I am!
I the person, a real being, gone!
Who shall snatch me out of this fateful bondage?

Jump ship, idiot!
Just jump off the ship
I, the soul, the owner of my life, say that
I do it

RANCHO PARK

The waves of the two-footed beasts
In foursome with the bags of steel sticks
Tramp through Rancho Park day after day
For a man-vs-nature bout
The beast wielding the stick
Fires shot after shot
At the angels to bleed Red
But, few see the Red

The eighteen angels of nature
Defend the Lore of the course
The angels poach the pride
Slay the ego of the beasts
Send them home with the bags full of bogeys

Along came a legend of golf, Arnie, with his own army
To challenge the angels guarding the course
One of the angels got him
At the eighteenth hole and slew him
With the twelve bruises on his face, and
Turned his cheering army into the shock
For his defeat here
A tombstone was erected
To comfort the mortals coming to the hole

Rancho, amid the lushes of the city and the pushes of man
Thou art great
Over thy turf, few eagles soar
The flock of birds hovers above man's head
Thou art serene
The trees dance in the open sky
Peeking beneath at man's whim and wrath
Thou art rock-solid, and
Sucks the fuss and flurry of man like
The Black Hole
Thou humbles the arrogance of man
Ode to thee
Thou shall be evermore
Even after man is gone for good

THE DIFFERENCE

The difference between man and nature
Lies in the innate
The Big Bang wrapped
Man into the two bags; of Mind and of Body
Matter just into one bag: of Nature/body

Man roves from the bag of Nature onto
The bag of Mind through a thin lifeline
Body peacefully abides
In the care of Nature
While Man is pulled toward the Center by Reality
Where Nature is
He is pushed outward where
Mind wants to wander off

The similarity between man and matter
Is in the relationship
The body of man exists when tended by the mind
Even as an atom needs to be observed to exist
Man is called a being
For he is not yet even an entity, but always
In the process of becoming one

He is between Mind and Body
The body boards life; but

The mind eats that life to build its own dream house, and
Drives the body into the fatal coil
He is torn in the duo's constant duels, and
Is in peril, and cries out
"Oh!, wretched man that I am."
Help, help, and help till the breath runs out

The Bag of Mind, art thou the lore of man? Or
Art thou just empty to the core? Or just
A wind blowing in void now and then, here and there?
I know thee not
Except that thy interests in things lush so fast, and
Thy intrigues intensify, so the Bag now bursts open
Thou becomes the unbound, open field without fence or gate
Thou teems with lust
The body hardly contains thee

THE MOUNTAIN & THE SELF

To climb up the mountain
Is to free the self from
The earth-bound mundane with the mind

I could honor the spirit
Unbuckled, elevated onto the light
In the fresh air
The spirit floats freely
The heart breathes the same air
The two tango singing
A song of the being

The foxy mind, which dogs the being
Has been ditched
Into the pit below for now

Behold: wing I the being
Through the heavenly sky
With a fuel tank full of happiness
Let the mountain salute, and
Let the valley adore

MAN

A BYPASS SURGERY

I is the capital letter, and it happens to be
The captain of my ship
The I toils the waves of the mind, and the heart
Totters between the two
The agents of the world pollute
The field of the mind like a mine field of battles
But the heart wants to sing the song of angels

My being is at stake
My life is at risk
Let a bypass surgery be performed on me
To take out the mind
Which has been the bane of my existence
Undermining the I

Bury that mind deep, chained under the shadows of
Freud, Nietzsche, and mind masters
Let it never return to my being again
Cut off its legs, so that it never walks
Chop off its hands, so that it never touches me
Pluck out its eyes, so that it never sees me

The I is now free, and courts the heart
The two tango
Singing the song of life, and
Becoming one in the being

A DART IN THE DARK

No more than a dart in the Dark
Wobbling in thick dusts of the dark Cave
And yet, no less than a being to be
That is what I am

I am indeed nothing but
Just a wobbling dart in the black cave
Between the left and right
I am utterly confused
More chaos than order
Where is the symmetry?
Asymmetries abound
In the wilderness of the human mind!
My mind dwells on the street floor
The more it tries to steer to the order
The worse it gets to the chaos

Of late, after fourscore long journey
I have found out the mind had been
The emissary of the world
The lateral search fails
No more trust in the things of the world!

AN AGED SONG STUDENT

An old man, but young in heart
Is learning new songs; discovers
The language of heart through music
He had indeed spent more than three score years
In fiddling with the language of head

He now fiddles his own heart
To sing songs of love
Ecstatic over this new tool for expression
Rejoices in singing
He forms a trio: soul, heart, and head
Conducts the performance
It is indeed a heavenly art in singularity!

Heart is a better communicator of love
Head is only good for arguing and aggressions
Is rarely attuned to love
But, love feeds, heeds, revs up the heart
The two are the eternal couple
Bonded in essence
The soul, though quieted by the flesh
Reigns in the loop

The old song student sings the songs of love
As if he were playing a flute
Using his windpipe
Rather, he lets the heart thus play
The intricate part for singing

AN ORANGE TREE AND ME

In my backyard, the orange tree gloats with
A few bright oranges
Still surviving only on its high branches
The winter sun had just overcome the morning shade
Killed the chills in the air
The tree and I are basking in the sun

A paradise lurks in a corner of my mind
The I of the being that reins in the subject-object field
Sees the picture; beauty is extracted!
For this sudden flame of beauty
I want the time out; shrink the world into
A small picture of the tree, and me, and the sun
That snapshot sewed onto the mind
Everything else vanishes!

And now, I clasp the tree and climb a little to reach the orange
Which lures my eyes with delicious color
My healthy nails, dexterous fingers, and clever tongue
All work the orange into my body
From skinning the orange to eating it to taste
A delicious warm spark in the cold of reality
For the height of serenity

What then there is reality?
Is the tree more real than the sun?
For I see, touch, and even taste it?
I must be more real than the picture
Since I beheld it, and still hold it now
In my gray clay under skull
And, nothing can be more real than me
Except my own Creator

Hopping back to the time zone, and
Crawling back into the Cave
I realize how little I know beyond
These immediate realities. But, who cares!
That I exist and live a happy life is good enough for me
The less I know, the simpler I become, and
The better my life
The light still shines within me
Enlightens the different components in me;
To be a whole being, which matters most

BEING SEEN AND HEARD

Man loves to be seen and heard
He could sell anything he can grab
And, indeed, sell even his own soul
To attract attention
All for the showing
To the world of Extensions
Alas. A moppet dancing
In the midst of the moppets
Without Substance; Nor with Subject
Death to the being of the individual!

But, from the prospective of a sensible
Feeling person, the world
Is two-faced: virtual and sensible
Only in the sensible world
A real life would be lived
And could feel a sense of existing
Beyond the tangled web of
Existential extensions

Let Substance become Subject
Let Spirit court Mind
To be one
All united
Tango with Beauty
Good ensues
For the inner serenity
Of the being

BETWEEN SUBJECT AND OBJECT

Beyond the grammar
Above the semantic
Am I a subject only of the whole entity?
Interacting with a multitude of objects
Whirling and spiring inside the Whole?
Am not I an agent free to crawl out,
And crawl back into the Whole
To suit the mode of my own being
And, thus creating my own invisible loop
For existential survival?

A life lives not just in the between
But also beyond the relationship
Of subject and object
Even beyond the sensible world itself
The life licks the subject that speaks
The language of a living being
But, kicks it when flirting with the world
It refuses to be encroached by
An object being promoted by the world
For his individual decency and integrity

I am only a being
That I am, is being made
In the very present, and ever more

In the Process; never complete
Nor finished: permanently framed
In the Process toward Good
Till the sensible world
Disappears from me altogether
With my very last breath

BEYOND SPACE AND TIME

Unable to possess my yesterdays
Nor to access my future
As ever, I am reduced to Now
Which is not a dot in the Flux
But where eternity is born and rejoiced

Let my yesterdays sink
Into a black hole, and my tomorrows
Into a bright hope, and
Leave me just at the Now, where my being
Is being born and renewed to be at my best

Pristine and true
Behold the being at its summit
Happiness suddenly embraces the being
Like a mother cuddling her baby

THE JOY OF SINGING

Wooh, woo, the wind blows
Whipping trees; the fallen leaves
Scatter, littering the black sky
And then, and now, dead quiet
A chilly autumn night
Bundled-up folks hurry homeward
As the naked trees along a narrow road
Look on

The blood-soiled moon above limps
Through the patchy clouds
Up, up, over the mountain

Now back in home
I warm myself up in front of the fireplace
Suddenly, all out of the blue
I feel good, so good as if
The weight of death is lifted
From the wings of my soul
The soul longs to whisper
In a mystic tune: ho, ho, ho; ha, ha, ha
A happy tone from out of the world

Sing along. Sing loud, my soul
Ever louder. Let the joy of singing

Gush out, and overwhelm the self
I rejoice in the harmony and
In the serenity of my whole being
Long, long live the soul!
Forever and ever

OF FIRST PERSON

The most spoken word, and yet
The least understood, is I
Philosophers dig into it
Preachers frame it
Punks spit it out
Poets play with it

It is this i that the first person
Played like a trump card before the world
He invents it before his every statement
It is the great masker in the art of hiding behind the face
The best showman in front of an audience
The master of dual roles either for good or evil

Even before a thing is conceived
An i was already begotten in the mind
What gave birth to it?
Could an I be born of the root?
To ply the life of the subject for good
Or, just born of the mere object for whim?

The cubs multiply and wilt the mother
Many are in the ring to claim the throne of the mother
The cubs spin a web wishing to catch the source

The soul, the final source, cries out for life
Who is that says that I am
Or, says that I exist?

Few build a bridge between the winks
Of the being and the wiles of the world
Essence of existence is as simple as I is, but
Elusive as human mind
To be and to live is, never to be the question, but
The answer capital I seeks, while the life
Dangles down between the two:
The self and the world

EXISTENCE

A BIRD VIEW

The tomb-shaped, windowless church,
Stands on the cold concrete
A large man-made cross hung high
Beneath, man's odors hover
Theirs mix with the summer's hot air like
A pressure keg
Bound by the past and programmed
In its old traditions, men and women
Sit on the rows of the pews like manikins
A newly arrived pastor batters the way
Trying to blow Words
Into their waxed ears

Nearby looms a mortuary with a large gate
The Deads are ushered into the dark pit morgue
Few mourners are seen
Obituary speeches are hardly heard

Beyond, and way above the dirt and the flesh
In the deep blue sky
A family of mockingbirds
Looking on from the high wire
Boast serenity, and sing hymns in peace

IN THE NOW

I live today
As the air flows in and out of my lungs
I love today
As if there were no yesterdays nor tomorrows
I laugh at my yesterdays, and
Let the tomorrows just flow into me

If today is to be and to live
From Then and Hence
Come I onto the Now
In which the root of my being grows
I matter only in that very present
As I am void on the past
Futile for the future

Death has many faces
So does life many names
But, I have no address
Nor carry I any label
I earn my being in the Now
Even as my blood travels to, and
From the remotest part of my body
I hold my flesh and bones

Onto the Center so as to be in unity
In the Now I am all together
I live today
I exist
In the Now

"JUNG"?

Is "Jung" a derivative of Romeo &Juliet' love?
Wrong.
Is it written with the red hot blood of Son of Man?
Wrong.
Did jiggy Freud, the king of sex theories, invent it?
Wrong.
It is not even a name of Western mind masters.
It is a product of the East.
Yes.

Have you ever seen a farmer of the East
Radiating the love of the soil and the village?
Or have you ever heard of a widow of the East
Mourning her dead husband for life?
Love in the West has width and extent.
But its depth and duration endure in the East.
It is the representation of the mind in the West.
The love in the East sinks through, and
Stays below the mind.
It trickles into the blood stream, and called
"Jung", that is a kind of immersed love-attachments
Flowing out from the depth of a heart through time.

NO MORE YES

Yes to the left
I follow my ego's whim, and
Race to be ahead and above
I become a vain city man

Yes to the right
I fill my belly, and
I am bloated like a tadpole
I am a member of the pig farm

Yes to the head
I am intrigued by the world, and
My spine is over stretched to the tomorrows
I am blurred of reality

Woes to them all
The hands, the head, and
The delicate parts, which all partake
In the plays of the"i"s in the absence
Of my being the "I"

No more yes
Blot out all the yesterday's yeses, and
Remove all the "i"s of the yesman from me
Return me naked to my boyhood
I shall salute to my heart, and
Tune in to its beats

ONE DAY AT A TIME

Everyday, I preach to myself
For living one day at a time
The unruly mind defies
Drifts away, leaves me alone
Instead of living fully together
In the very moment

Where does that restive thing called
Mind wander off?
Onto the things past, things yet to happen
Or, utterly out of the time frame itself
Poor me that I am
This very idiot happens to be
The driver of my own life
Poor my soul at the mercy of
This elusive, restless idiot

A dream has but one owner
So does a life only one
An atom can not be
Two different places at once
Nor one can be in two different states
In the same moment
Nature dictates either this or that

Life is already dreadful enough
But, lived fully one day at a time
Even better yet, each moment
Filled with hope for eternity
It begets joys
As the hope kicks the dread
Fears fade away. Then, only then
Peace, into which soul, mind, and body
Converge for the being

OUT OF THE CAVE

I am a many-headed animal tamed in the cage
Built with the iron will
But, the wall of the cage is sturdier than the will
My flesh dwells in the cage
Located in the large dark cave beneath the earth

The two wings my heart has
One on the left side, the other on the right
Each has a separate center, and
The two are, rarely, in sync
Only in love we are all united and
We become one and fly together
Even in and out of the cage
The heart whispers to the wind
About the dream it had the night before
And flirt with the tall palms trees of the earth
Dancing in the deep blue sky of the autumn

Not only out of the cage
But also out of the cave itself
Beyond the reach of time and
Outside of space altogether
I am free

I am utterly free like a spirit
From the human bondage
I am free at last
Alas! I have overcome the world
My heart rejoices ever more

PEACE IN THE BEING

Men may take my name tag from the chest and
Put it up higher to the eye or head levels.
Would they add anything to my being?

Men may pull it from me altogether and
Throw it into the trash bag
What could they do to my being?

Men may get rid of all my things
Is my being to be reduced to non-being?

Men may cheer me up or tear me down.
Is my being to alternate accordingly?

Men may tempt me to the things of this world
What would I gain for my being?

What then is my being?
It is the home of a spirit that owns my life

Let the men of war have the spoils
For I love peace over all things, and
I have no barn to hoard them anyway

It is the being versus the thing
It is the being that
Matters only in the being
Where the spirit resides
Like the mind lives in the flesh

REALITY: WHAT IS IT?

What is reality: art thou the pronoun?
For all things under the sun
Or just an invisible bag containing all appearances?

From subjective perspective, it could be
Only a fleeting shadow of the collective images
Of the hearts and the minds
As the mass worship the world

The world is a massive magnet
Begets states, gangs, groups, and the likes
Bewitching the people to gravitate to it
Woe to that Whole for all the miseries
Of the modern man

Brief, so brief that all blur and fuzzy
Like in a drunk dream
Is this world, which
My naked eye see, real?

Maybe only a world of the mind
False creation
Proceeding from the fear-driven brain
Fears rule the mind

Tears wet the heart
Wearing down to death
The soul weeps

The pains and perils abound in the bondages
Vanity of vanities; vanity of all vanities
"The eye is not satisfied with seeing
Nor the ear filled with hearing:"
Seduced and reduced to nothing!
All is indeed vanity
A whole bag of vanity!

Reality is only a relationship thing between
The eye and object; and depends on the eye to perceive
To stare at nothing is to learn by heart
What the whole is doing to us all
Barring one to the wind of the whole
Is feeling the ungraspable power of it

RE-LIVING MY CHILDHOOD

My Christmas is here once again
At the end of the Millennium
The Christmas tree soars to the ceiling
The motley lights shine over the colorfully wrapped presents
Piled up under the tree

Hallelujah!
I relive my childhood through my grandchildren
I rejoice in the real love I sense in the air
As I open the gifts. I feel the warmth
Of love all over
I even smell the hands of Love

Hallelujah!
I love the Christmas like a child
I am indeed a child born again in love
The joys of a childhood seeps through my body
I play with the toys with the kids. I love them as friends
From the kids I am just learning to love
I pray for them to grow in God's Love

Hallelujah!
I thank God for sending the Savior for all of us
I am grateful to my Lord preserving me until now
I shall let the glow of Love, and

Live and shine throughout the year and beyond
In love always
I shall grow up with the glow of the spirit

I shall chant: my God my love. I shall keep chanting
My God my life, my God my all
Until the last breath of my flesh

Hallelujah

A grandpa Inspired
By the grandchildren

THE SINGULARITY

Who art Thou?
Wants to settle the War
Between Matter and Mind for good
For Humanity
Beyond the equations of
Relativity and Quantum

As the last locomotion of Humanity
Thou art lurking from the time capsule
Daring to supersede God and the Man
With a new Mankind
Formatted and Digitized
Man and machines are merged
Being amalgamated into One Whole
Which is called
Singularity

Alas!
Beauty, Good and love:
The pillars of the individual being for Happiness
Dumped out
Onto the backyard of the Whole
The Whole now stalks and wades freely
The private courtyard of the individual person
Making it barren
Beheading the human happiness

Woes onto the Singularity!
Thou murders the individuality of the man
Thou enslavest the whole of humanity
Thou art destined to be
The last syllable of recorded time
The end of Time
And no more space

THE TEARS

The blood, still warm
Mixed with the hot black oil that was
Spilled from the cars
That were just crushed in a freeway collision
Was flowing over
The cold concrete pavement

The traffic resumed
Pushing aside the tragedy of the death
To the passing cars
The death never occurred
Even the screaming of the injured was not heeded
Only dying off in the roaring din of the night traffic

The dead had the eyes wide open
But the unprepared owner of the body
Had left for the unknown
Leaving only the tears
On his blooded face

THE CAVE

I was living in a cave carved out deep in Space
Away from the flurry and fury of Man, and
Beyond the Time Zone
The cave was decked with gold from the Bible
Decorated with silver lines from great books
Lighted by wisdoms from East and West
Walled with tough-run will
Out of the world indeed
Most perfect place for a monk
Who constantly meditates a different world!

Back in the time zone, by a sudden unknown will
My head fell off to the chest as though
My neck was chopped off
I that I was, wake to the lore of Love
Even as I am headless
Alas, my system
It crashed!
The debris falling onto the palm of the heart

Do away with that fox hole
Stop eating the fake of faith. And
Start to have a real cake made of love

A life blooms on the files of love
For love is the cause and source of life

Feast the life on love
For love connects
Toast to the love
For it is mightier than
All the powers of this world combined
Brighter than all the lights put together
Only Love can lift a life onto the higher plane
Where Truth shines

THE CHRONIC CRISIS

The life in the chronic crisis
Baring oneself to the whim of the mind
Is feeling the impulse of the moment
The reason can agree, or argue
The heart can inhale, or exhale
Feel hot or cold; happy or unhappy
Be that may
But, the crux of the matter
For the being
Is who that is in charge?

The life itself is at stake
The fear-filled mind drives the life
Often lingers
By the panic button
The whole show is staged on
The home base, which stands
On the quicksand

The life is in the mode of
The chronic crisis: reacting to
One incident to the next
Or, event to event
Befalling to that existence

The life driven by
The freewheeling mind
Is worse off than one
Secured in a prison cell

THE SECRET SMELL

The hunting dog can distinguish
The smell of its master's prey
From the whiff for its own appetite
And, even remember the odors of
The path of the trip for
Their safe return home

But, man's nose is keyed only
To his appetite, which is
An aspect of his desires
When lost in the wilderness
Of desires, his nose, too, gets lost
Let alone find the way home

Baring oneself to the whim of desires
Is feeling the unfolding of something close by
Trees can sway or be still
The wind can blow this or that way
What man wants is the comfort
Of being his ways, always

To sense nothing at all, even by the nose
Is to learn by heart
The beauty of smells themselves
When all the senses are so aligned

As to give the soul to reign over the being
The secret smell sneaks into the home
Of its own accord
Sweeter than ready lips
Purer than a newly born
And, beyond human tastes

THE TARES

In me tares grow
Sucking the good onto which
I barely cling for my being
Daily my hands get bloody
Fighting them off for my survival

In my dream I beg the Lord
For the weed killer
I wake up every morning
Without it, and start my battle
With my bare hands

I now manage to let the tares
Co-exist side by side
With the good
That I am able to keep
And I learn how to be

I understand why
I was created this way
Rather than my way
The idea of weed killing
Vanishes from me

THE WHOLE

On the prairie of life
There is a large prison, indeed
Larger than life, but smaller than history
Where all the inmates are serving life sentences
The prison is lighted day and night
Sun or Moon need not pass over it
For the motley prisoners bask
In the brightness of man-made light

At the center, high above Earth
The huge Magnet stands tall, which
Binds the minds of the prisoners
The Magnet transcends the minds
Within the sphere of the Magnet
The bodies roam freely, while the particles of
The minds amalgamate to form the whole
The prison is called the Whole
For all in it have become the parts

Nature nags the Whole for tinkering the way of man
Sends its emissaries for rapprochement
Sun swirls about it day after day
Moon smiles on it month in month out
Wind whispers to it every season
The chorus of angels sing Fate without ceasing
Nature wants to coexist with man

The trinity of God, Nature, and Man
Has been replaced by the whole
The whole now grows and
Glows blighting on the grave of the trinity
The whole immortalizes the cells of the bodies
To make the parts even stronger, and
Dumps the souls on the outer edge
To make the minds even weaker

It is thus the story of man
Withering on the vine
Who never returns
Home again to the land of the living

TIME

A hair falls from the forehead
Into the palm
Barely touching the skin
Time had bleached it
It is now as white as fair, and
As light as a spirit

Time manufactures tomorrows
Using todays
Time ticks, kicking the nows away
It murders the presence
It is the eternal foe of man
For it deprives him of the stable being

It stashes all the yesterdays into building
The jail to house man
Time allures man with
Its bait made of tomorrows, and
Blenches the mind like
It had done to the whiten hair

TODAY IS SANDWICHED

Today is sandwiched between
Yesterday and tomorrow
The tomorrow sucks the juice
Of the current day, and
The yesterday yelps at it
It is being yelled and abused
In the middle
The Today is
A battle ground
For a happy life now

Oh, my poor current day!
Thou art being robbed by the past
Thou art being misled by the future

It is the Mind that defiles
Time and Space
Freely traverse on the time scale
And even beyond
Deep into the weird world of
Imaginations and abstracts
The soul sobs at
The whims and wickedness
Of the Mind,
Which is free from the Body
Free at large, indeed

I VS THE WORLD

Out, out, I kick the Mind out
Out of my being in the Now
The very now of my current time
Never again mess with the Mind
Oh, my soul
Never leave me alone
In the Now of the day

Brave it out all for the being
I moor my being in the Now

LOVE

A SOLDIER OF LOVE

The sound of love calms my nerves
The sight of love stirs my heart
The power of love overcomes me altogether
Hallelujah. I love Tres Dias
The savor of love touches my soul
Hallelujah. I love Love Tres Dias
Love wakes me up to the Lord

Oh Lord, here come I to Thee
What shall I do?
I am in Love
I am full with Love
I am ready for Love
Hallelujah
Joys spring; Tears sparkle
Wipe off my tears, Lord. And
Enlist me into Thy Army
Arm me with a rifle of love

Let my tongue shoots Hallelujahs
Let my hands deliver the cares of Love
Let my legs walk the works of Love
I shall march on
As a soldier of Love
I shall march on, onto the fields of life

I shall raise the flame of Love high
I shall sing the songs of Love loud
I shall march on onto the end
I shall keep marching on
Until the last breath of my flesh

PS: This piece was composed during a Tres Dias session at Big Bear(Nov., 1998) to dedicate my commitment to Love, and to thank to the Team Members and to LTD #26 Classmates.

ALL-IN-ONE FOR A LIFE

Of a life, love is the linchpin
Love is an essence for a being
Love implements a life
As a being breathes love to exist
Even more vital staple

As for the mind
Love is the only power
Fatal fissure in the mind
That can change and form into a shape

A human being is what he makes of himself
How is he going about making of himself?
Love changes a man
As love is a staple of life as air is to the body
And defragment the mind
Even affects the body over time

Love brings the mind and body together
Unify them into a full happy being

Love is all in one for the existence
And is the perpetual mother of all the beings

AN EPISODE

An ugly American trapped in Seoul subway toilet
Cried out for help
He had just discharged before reaching the toilet, and
Messed up the underwear and pants
He was helplessly wrapped with his own wastes

A spectator's hands debated the head
To help the naked stinking stranger out
Or to just pass by
As the skin-piercing odor shook his spine
The hands wanted no touch. But
The head needed a good deed
The hand told the legs: go, find a pair of pants for the man
But, failed to find his size, which was out
Of the range on the Land
Finally, the head took charge and asked
The hands do the work

The hands, which happened to be yellow in skin color
Started removing the white man's shits from the pants
When it was all cleaned
The ugly American hurriedly covered himself
Into the wet pants and quickly
Escaped being seen even uglier

The hands, head, legs all joined together
In rejoicing of the job well done, and saluted to
The whole that coordinated the team work
In achieving unity for good

ENGRAVING A LOOP

One thinks of life as a journey
From birth to death
In a life-long journey
Along the way to the dead end
An object-driven life for the senses

Wait. And rethink
There is a different way of life
Stay tuned to the inner voice of the self
Hoist the being up high, and orbit it
Around the Truth
Engrave the orbital track for the being
Live in that loop under the skull
In a soul-directed life for the Truth

What, then, is at stake?
The being: That is
The very core of life itself
But, it is an indeterminate
Yet most immediate, entity
A work-in-process
Being formed and developed
In the present, and through
The deeds of loving

In the real time
Loving to be
I love, therefore I am

Derailed from the loop of love
Or, without the being
Engaged in earnest
I, then, adrift
Whine, wither, and die

FOR THY LOVE

For thy love
Purge my mind, and
Purify my blood
For thy love
Let that love be the food of my existence

For thy love
Purge my mind, and
Purify my blood
For thy love only
My soul may grow for thy love

Again, for thy love
Purge my mind, and
Purify my blood
I shall repeat again and again
Till that Love comes and resides in me for good

HOW DO I LIVE LIFE?

How do I live life - in the journey of doing things?
Or in the joy of being
Or in the juggling the two?
To be, or to do: the question lingers on
Where do I get a manual for living a life?

Inside the cave of the Whole
I watch my own shadow dimming on the wall
The Whole matters here; it fleshes up
By leaching men even as they worship it
Its limelight kills all the shadows of the individuality within
Illuminates the Logo symbolizing its value
It fills the air with its own incense

Lo, mere dust that I am; just a cell of the whole!
At the expense of my being
I become a perpetual part of that mass
As time eats eternity
The becoming beats the being
In the name of the whole
Reality emerges, and Truth submerges

I jump ship over to the kingdom of Love
From the ever entangling web of the mind
Operating in my left cerebral hemisphere

Over to the right side and onto the fertile field of the heart
Where life blooms in Love
Love erases pain and elates existence
It never fails
I find the existential manual
In the treasure of Love

I JUST FEEL LOVE

Higher than heaven
Deeper than earth
Wider than space
That is
Love

Better than the things of man
More than the quantity of his measures
Loftier than any honor of the man
That is
Love

Mightier than the power of a conqueror
Stronger than the hatred of a woman
Larger than the life of any giants
That is
Love

Softer than the smile of an innocence
Serener than the peace
Purer than the spirit
Holier than the hope
Even greater than Faith
That is
Love

In the serenity of its beauty and power
Richer than the wealthiest
Taller than the highest
Happier than the happiest
I feel that
I am

IF I CAN

If I can help a white to see a black
I shall rejoice in Love

If I can build a bridge of love between a black and a yellow,
I could show it also to between a black and a white

If I can bring a black and a white together
I shall rejoice in peacemaking

Love is color-blind, but
Love brightens every color
Diversity grows only in love
And beautifies the nature
Makes life richer
Love is therefore the most potent for life
No cold can freeze it
Nor any heat can dry it up
Love is the cause and the juice of life
The eternal source for life
Let a life be color blind
And just live in love

THE LITTLE THINGS OF LIFE

Mind would love to possess big things
Like a pile of money; or would sit on
A heap of honors, or
Just to carve out a place in their midst
For these passions of the world
Mind thus leaves the little things of life
Behind on the ground
As if they are not needed
Vanity: All is vanity
Big is ugly

The real caviar of life is
The little things on hand like
A small bowl of noodles
To the hungry mouth
Or, a feeling of subtle warmth
In a happy hug
A few bills in the pocket to pay for lunch
Are immediate and concrete
Therefore, more real than
A large sum of money on paper
Small is beautiful

Love seeks a loop built
With the little things. And there

The love flows through it
Life is real and rich
Only with love. Again with love
The life blossoms into emitting
The aroma of life
Beauty emerges!

LOVE: LINEAR VS LOOP

Love is like a wind
That touches the skin
And passes away
But, true Love
While the body may miss
The spirit surely senses it

Love is real
Pushing and pulling a life
To be a being
Lifting it up high to see beauty
As well as keeping the self in the being

Is love then like a substance?
For a life
Beyond the body
Even within the body
Never sensible

A linear love is an object-driven
Eccentric force toward the world
While the true loop love is a subject-driven
Concentric power circling
The core of the self

LOVE

Fears cease
As love is lit

Tears sparkle
As joy lifts the spirit

Peace shines
As faith grows

Love wins always
For it overcomes all things

THE MAN AND LOVE

Love is many things
Has many faces
She is homeless, hiding in different places
Discrete as a spoiled child
When grabbed, flees
When possessed, never returns
And yet, she is everywhere
Is the center and circumference of the world?
Framed in by the dual flames of love and hate
Love is as diverse as a cosmopolitan city

Man gropes a spell of love
Dreaming of becoming beloved
Routs each other in pursuit of it
The young touts the flesh
Licks the paw of love for a smell of sex
And yet, Love vexes many

But, the old rejoices in the wisdom of love
Is reborn to be a lover
A lover of Love
Blessed is a lover!
Love now comes to him, and stays with him
For he is wiser, tender, caring for her

The lover beholds her Beauty
Feels her presence
She is greater than life itself
And is the soul's mate
Even has a domain over the death

MY BRAT

The naivety of her childhood still dwells
In her sparkling eyes
A few wrinkles and scars on her body
Have yet to win over her recklessness
Watch her walk
Listen to her talk
Joys pop up
Out of her deep dimple on her left effortlessly

Sorrows are pushed into tomorrows
Pains are left to the body
She lives today
As if in the fantasy of a brat
She begets brat-like acts all the times
She is indeed a brat herself
She shall never be otherwise
Leave her alone
Let her nature run its course

The brat I met three generations ago
Is today still the same
I love her this same steadiness
For she has now become
A vital part of my own being

MY FIRST & LAST JOY

My journey unto the wilderness of the world
Began with Joy
She was a little lily of the valley
I was a young hart

I wandered in the wilderness
Without a map or a guide
To seek my way to be
I strayed into the swamp land of things
I veered to the left, and
Steered back to the right, searching to fill my void
I found none
Nothing but vanity, all was vanity
Always was vanity
Truth eluded me
Beauty hid from me
A wretched man that I became!

Now that I am home again where Joy continues to be
Like the Tree in the Quad
I come to the sense of my self
As Truth reigns in me

I am free
Even to see Beauty
I now see Joy through the window of Beauty
She is my first joy and
My last Joy

MY TRIBUTE TO LOVE

A love for the ages
The love that bloomed for
The least: the lepers of Korea
Condemned to perish by their own people
On a secluded island, Sorokdo
A leper colony of the country

A love lived there by two nuns
From the Downunder caring and nursing
The lepers for scores of years
The love lived for no return
A towering example
Of real love for God

They spent their entire life
Risking their own existence
Almost anonymously
A heaven-piercing deed!!

May God bless and adorn them
Loving God, therefore they were there
Live forever in the Spirit

I just adore their endearing sacrifice
For the most unfortunate humans

On this planet
It chills my spine
My heart shivers
I salute the beauty of their Love

OF A LOVER OF THE LOVE

The word "love" is one of the most commonly
And frequently used by the mankind; as it
Triggers happy emotions like no other word
And yet
Nevertheless, never fully
Man lives the love as fully
As it allows the being to be

The world begets the beloved out of its womb
Ceaselessly, and is teeming all with them
Inside the big Sphere, consisting of
Two hemispheres: one on the left
The other, on the right
The beloved dwell only in the Left
Worship the world day and night
At the Altar of the great Edifice

The beloved is, nevertheless, always in want
Desiring to be free and be a whole; and wishes to be
United with the love for good
When the cheering roars wane, the applauses die
And the Stadium lights are off
She cries alone in the depth of darkness
And lies low on her own dunghill

Now here
Enter a lover. The world knows him not
Nor has a place for him
Without a tag, he begs from place to place
Hoping to deliver the love
To the beloved: but she knows of it little
The lover has pity for her ignorance of him
And sympathizes with her perils and pains.

After a day's work of the love, he returns
To his home in the Right hemisphere
Where the love perks him up
He is full, and lacking nothing
And rejoices in the being of a whole
Love flows in, and out of him effortlessly
Blessed be the lover of the love
For he is a partaker of the Divine Process

SALUTE MARRIAGE

Who think that the love of Romeo and Juliet died in Shakespeare?
Who think that old-fashioned love is a by-gone thing?
Who think that the kernels of Love and Truth are not the same?

Love is God's and shall never perish
Like Truth
It's the essence of life
In the wonderful world of love
Everything under the sun converges
For all things commence from love
Love is above and beyond good and evil

Evil routs
Good revives. And
Love establishes and enhances
Ensures a being for existence
As imperative for the being as air is for the body
It sustains life
In Love

Life flourishes in love like
Trees grow and glow in the sunlight
Love brings good things
Peace and serenity
Love begets beauty
For it opens the eye to see

Today, we gather together here to salute
A fruit of this love: The marriage of Peter and Karen
I have watched these two young lovers grow, and
I see them now glow in the joy and happiness
Of their union
May this marriage last forever
Bring rejoicing to them unbounded

THE BLOOD OF LOVE

Love is in my blood
Running. It runs through all the loops
In my systems. It is real
As real as the air coming in
Through my nose
It makes me feel good

In the world, man chases after
The goods, and dreams to be a beloved
He becomes spoiled, and addicted
Unable to reign them in, and falls into
The abyss of the desires of this world
He perishes
The dream sinks with him
To the bottom of the pit

No, no, no to that hopeless fate!
I shuffle off this mortal coil, and
I choose to live as an active, and independent agent
Seeking the fullness of life in and out of the world
I would rather be a lover
For I know that a lover can see beauty, and
Reach truth. I am desperate to be, and to be a lover
I am convinced that I still can grow
To be a lover, even at an old age

Who can change my diverse natures and
Bad habits into harmony
Sync with the world
I put my all into Love to be a true lover

I praise Love, which is the bedrock of being
Love is in my blood running and
Cleansing each cell of my body
In the every passing moment of my life
Love frames thoughts and acts, and
Subjects my inner process to Truth
I let it flow through me freely
I owe love my being and body
By love I consist
I love therefore I am

THE FEET

I now follow my feet
Where the love needs me and
I pour my passion over
I walk on the soil sowing love
For others to reap

In solitude above the Flux
I hear the sound of my footsteps
I feel it real
I realize my being here and now, and
That I live

While the feet move forward
The mind alternates between
The now and the then
The mind repents that
It has abused the feet for so long
So far as to forget their existence

Now, the repentant mind lets
The feet lead to where
The love stays for good
The passion for Truth prevails
And I am whole again
Free at last

THE HUMAN DESPAIR

The human despair
Slowly seeps into a reflective mind
Over the realization
Of its inability to be a living entity that sees
Beauty and Good; and
Becomes a lover of Truth
As the staple of life

The mind gropes for itself
In its deeper swath in vain
As it eludes from being groped like
The particle disappearing when observed
It fails to understand the self
Nor to find the path to it
In the dark cave of Gray Matter
It never sees the light of life

The Mind can fool even the smartest
To make the Cartesian error, and
Cheat its own partners: soul and body
Become ever more clever
In manipulating them
In the self-dealing with the world, and
Relegate them to a minor role
Pierce the heart with a dagger

It could quickly turn even to be
A self-annihilating atom bomb!

Wretched mind that it is!!
It is the black hole of Sin
Sucking down everything around it

How can I show and prove to the mind that
There is a way up to peace and love
While the world teaches men to be a beloved?
And yet
All men are madly in the rat race for being loved

But, the twinkling light of Love
Celebrating the season, invites us
To be a lover; rather than to be a beloved
For only to a lover
Into whom the real power of love flows
Enlightening his whole being

THE LOWER, THE BETTER

A man with high aspirations
Seeks a vertical progress
Inside the sphere of the world
Like in a circus, performs acts in the high air
Seeking applauses from below
Which raises his ego even higher
He becomes tethered to the hot air of the sphere
Never leaves it till choked to death

But, consider a man
Whose existential perspective
Is firmly anchored on the ground
He walks freely and
Breathes the fresh air for his spirit
He is on the firm foundation
For building the home of his being

The lower he gets
The higher his spirit climbs
The better he becomes in loving all creatures
The more loving, the more the power
Of love for him

Lowering the self to the ground
Makes the spirit free and productive
Reigning on the Mind
Which is prone to court Matter
The spirit now is in charge
Of the whole being!

TO BE CHEAP, OR TO BE DEAR

Never be too cheap for love
Love has no absolute value as such
But in human relationship
Love is Imperative
In its dual functions
Cause and effect
Its value soars high to Heaven
And reaches deep into the hearts of men

It functions as a bonding agent
Not like drying glues
But ever soft and flexible
Like clay is to the pot maker
Loving is an art of sculpturing the self
On the wall of his heart
Its purpose is always noble
Between dignity and humility

The self plays his life with the love
Before the invisible Almighty
Not to show
But to sow his heart with love
And he reaps
The dearest of all things in life

UNLESS LIVED LOVING

Unless lived loving, I perish
Yes, I could live loving
And indeed I live loving
Even onto the death of my own ego
Life and love are so intimately
Linked, fatally interdependent
That only in the loving mode, I am alive
In the sense of the being

At the Divine Design
I just marvel!
The Creation's secret device for
Peace among the creatures
I am simply subdued
In realizing that I am only a creature
Subject to this law of Love

Lest seduced for being a beloved
I lie low to work the love
With the limbs
I sow the seed of the love

And reap abundantly; and
My cup runs over
I, therefore, live to be a lover
For all reasons; and
For all seasons

GOD

A LAMB

I am a lamb roaming freely
The land of wolves
Without fears
Daily, I lay up my meal on their silver plates
And, I earn my peace

I am a lamb roaming freely
The land of wolves
Without wants
For the Maker fills my gold cup with joys
And, my spirit rejoices

I am a lamb roaming freely
The land of wolves
In peace
For my Maker decorates me with stars
And, I am whole in Unity

I am also a spirit roaming freely
In and out of Matter
I have the two worlds on my palm

Hallelujah
The tears of joy sparkle reflecting
Love
The mouth shivers in
Thanking

A MEASURE OF FAITH

How do I measure my faith in God?
Having gone through many near fatal falls
I have now fired myself to be
The captain of my life-ship
No more trust in my own rationales
Goodbye to the idea of self-help
No more Cartesian dualism of mind and body
Beyond all these
Only God
He alone
Is all things and everything to me
As my savior
He does make me a happy and healthy person
Even well into the fifth score of years here on earth
I solemnly grant Him as a sole custodian of my life
Now and beyond

A PASTOR'S PASSING

The ashes of his pain
Descend on the congregation
Like fall rain, and
Mix with the scattered leaves

The arrows of his words
Still pierce through the skins
Of the members, and
Puncture the sorrow's bag

The season's chills chide with
Rolling hills of the valley
In black shadows and flickering light
The mourners shiver

Beyond the veil of time
From the pain to peace at last
He rises and rests on
Rose Hills

ALL NEW

Whipped by the tongue, and
Buried under the molten lava
I lie low like a turtle
Beneath its armored shield
Yet, I breathe as freely
As the spring air

Trashed away like rotten cabbages, and
Trodden down
I glue to Earth like the sludge
Out of the city sewage
Yet, I feel as safe
From men as the stars of heaven

I am a punching bag hanging down low
From the high beam
I am freely swaying in the air
As I am punched
As I am kicked. But
I return again and again to my position
As surely as the gravity of Earth

I mill my pride to powder and
Sprinkle them over the Garden of Vanity
Lest it return to vex my spirit

All day, I kill the warring members that are in me
Like in the final battle
I die many a death every day

From the ashes of my former lusts
My new life buds out
With the new food, and
The new air, and the all new
I live

BEAUTY: WHY HIDE THOU FROM MY EYE?

Beauty: why hide thou from my eyes?
Thou art hiding indeed from me altogether
I looked to the East; I found thee not
I searched the West; nowhere there, either
I, then, realized that I had misunderstood
The whole nature of it
That the beholding part was missing
I returned home for good
While I, the owner, was gone
Several wild tenants, who had claimed
To be the "I"es of the I themselves, must have lived in the house
I, the real owner, now assume full control of that home

Now, I began an inward search, combing
Through all the corners, studs and spaces of the house
All the way to the very core of my existential reality
"I "that is, now also am, a stranger to the house
The House has two stories plus an attic
The two-rooms upstairs; the left side room
Which is my study, has a limited view of the city
While the right room with a wide open view
Of the hills and the village, where I sing songs of life

My soul lives in the attic of that home
Where I have a hole in the roof
To see the sky; and to receive the morning dew
For my thirsty soul

The I subsists, therefore I live
I think of God in whom
I believe, therefore I am
And, Truth and Form emerge
Beauty unfolds
I only beckon

THE BONES

The ancient bones belonging
To the St. Paul: found and confirmed!
Alas and to my chagrin
Evil news ride post high
While this epochal good news bates

Who changed the landscape?
Of the hearts of men, and
By extension, the world itself
Who taught the Mind to be hearted?
Who persuaded that we are no good?
Without Love
St. Paul did

Martyred and buried in Rome
His words have been the best armor
Of the Heart against the ever assertive Mind
They trigger my emotion
Deep down to the bottom
I crush the words into my heart
For they wake the soul to rise; and
Whack the mind down to kneel
The midwife of Faith in
Truth and Love to Mankind

I almost feel as if the bones
Can speak to me
I would enshrine the bones
On the altar of my soul
For they were the real parts of
Apostle Paul the person himself then
Two millennium ago; and today
Even now he still remains shining
Ever more brightly for the Christians
All over the world as the guiding star
For their faith journey

SIN

Sin wraps me whole
Inside I bleed

I rather be naked
And be free

I am crossed altogether
In my own way

I stand naked
Before the Cross

PART III: HAIKUS

NATURE

Sweet spring rain sprinkles
Over the flower bed
The season smiles

A purple flower tree
Decorates the sky
Decomposed trashes on the curve

Icicles fall
The frightened birds fly away
The spring sun rises

Buds sneak out
Between the wrinkles of an old tree
The power of life

MAN

For the more of things
A man keeps toiling
Birds sing

The Bougainvilleas flourish
Even on dry hot lands
The barren mind

In the lush green tree
A bird rests in its nest
A man naps

In a room full of trophies
A man lies in states
The curtain falls

LIFE

Watching the dying
A child learns of life's end
Pains start

A man goes golfing
In the rain
The wife still in bed

With bloated belly
A man still enjoys eating
Wife decries

High with a substance
A man brushes with death
Powder keg

EXISTENCE

To be, or to have
A man choose to have
Sad soul

In the midst of crowd
A man feels lonely
The sign of modernity

To be seen
Man risks life
High price of being

With skills and knowledge
Mankind loaded
Virtue empty

REALITY

In a midnight romp
Sanity chokes
Pomp and vanity

With the numbing senses
Reality eludes the man
Death of realism

On the sand beach
A man leaves foot prints
Waves wash

Men straddle
Being and having
In the vanity village

HOPE

The sound of his own singing
He rejoices hearing
Proof of existence

The defect of man
Is God's default
I am just a work-in-process

Sacking the head
A man lets the heart drive him
Love of God

All things fading
In sight and memory
So is the idea of death

GOD

When all blinded
The world fades
God lights

The world seduces me
Into being its own part
God helps me to be my own whole being

Only living in the now
Death departs
God smiles

Mind and matter: the couple
Begets a being
God laughs

LOVE

For the being
To love is better than to be loved
A lover wins

Men love to honor
One another
Mutual promotion

Sling a smile
Even to a stranger
Joy of a lover

Sweet of love
Blows away the smell of death
Soft eternity

FAITH

In the house of fools
A drinking party is in full swing
The man next door meditates

A man lost in the whole
But found his own soul within
Freedom ticks

Clinching hope
A man clings to life
Birth of faith

Deeds alone
No salvation
Faith supersedes

GRACE

Man glued to the world's beats
Silences his heart
The soul seeks Grace

Desires to have suck the oxygen
But the desire to be a lover
Grace abounds

Conduct the mind
For harmony or for manipulation
Grace is over the mind

Brushing with sin
Bruises the conscience
Grace embraces

PART IV: ONTOLOGICAL GEOMETRY

QUARTER FIELD
for BEING

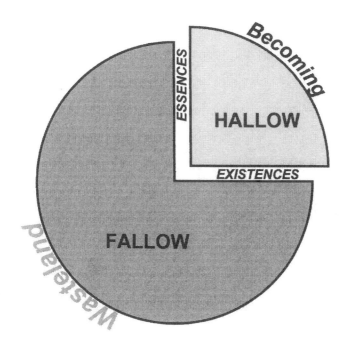

The "i" in Life

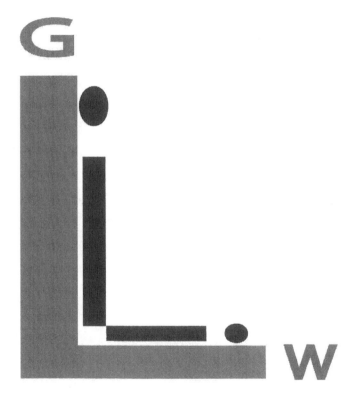

TWO HALVES

The "i" in Life

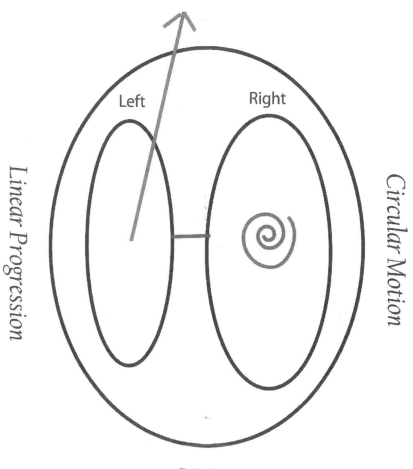

Twin in the Cave

Linear Progression

Left

Right

Circular Motion

It's me

165

Geometry of Being

Being = Y / X

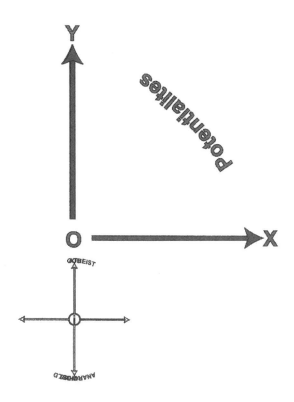

On Cartesian Coordinates

Process of Being

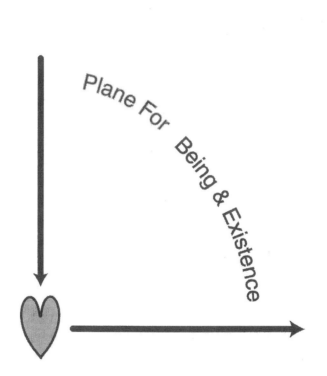

Plane For Being & Existence

The *Triangle*

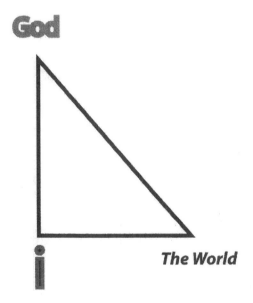

GRACE

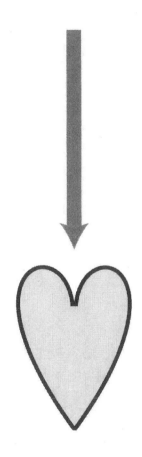

The "i" in Life

BIOGRAPH OF AUTHOR

Edward Sung Kyu Choi was born in Korea in 1931. A graduate of the Korean Military Academy (Class of 10th), he served in the Korean War and retired with a rank of Lieutenant Colonel at age 26 in 1957. He pursued higher education in the United States and earned a Master's degree in Economics from UCLA in 1962 after undergraduate study in History at Virginia Union University.

Edward worked as a securities analyst and a SEC-registered investment adviser. He has lived in Los Angeles, California since 1960; after retirement, reading the Love literature of East and West, and now writing his own poems as a devoted Christian.

28932397R00101

Made in the USA
San Bernardino, CA
10 January 2016